Rock Your Business!

Your Book as YOUR Business Card

By

Michael Ray King

Published by:
ClearView Press Inc.
PO Box 353431
Palm Coast FL 32164

Rock Your Business!
Your Book as YOUR Business Card

By Michael Ray King
Copyright © 2012 by Michael Ray King
All Rights Reserved
ISBN 978-1-935795-78-0

ClearView Press Inc.
PO Box 353431
Palm Coast FL 32135

mrking@clearviewpressinc.com
www.clearviewpressinc.com

Cover Design by Cynthia Lee Grudo
All Rights Reserved
cindyg@clearviewpressinc.com

All Rights Reserved. No part of this book may be reproduced, stored in a retrieval system, or transmitted in any form or by any means, electronic, mechanical, photocopying, recording, or otherwise, without permission in writing from ClearView Press, Inc.

Printed in the United States of America

Table of Contents

What is: Your Book as Your Business Card?	**- 1 -**
Marketing Tool	- 2 -
Oversized Business Card	- 3 -
Rich Content Business Cards Cannot Deliver	- 3 -
Book as a Prize	- 5 -
Income Stream/Marketing Tool	- 5 -
Speaking Engagements	- 6 -
Buy Product or Service – Get Book Free	- 8 -
Buy the Book – Get a Discount	- 9 -
Writing Your Book	**- 11 -**
Content is Key	- 11 -
Painting your Business Portrait	- 14 -
Writing the Innards	- 16 -
Book Layout	**- 24 -**
Getting Started	- 25 -
Setting Color and Print Resolution	- 28 -
Pagination	- 29 -
Cover Design	- 31 -
Publishing Model	**- 33 -**
Re-orders	- 34 -
ClearView Press Inc. History	**- 36 -**
Contact CVP	**- 39 -**
Books Published by ClearView Press Inc.	**- 41 -**

What is: Your Book as Your Business Card?

The concept of a book serving as a business card is not new. Avon has used this method for decades. Catalogs over the years have served many companies well. In this age of digital publishing, affordability levels the playing field for businesses and entrepreneurs who can make good use of a book that promotes their product(s) and/or service(s).

Today, business cards get passed around like bizarre playing cards, often falling into obscurity in desk drawers and trashcans. Even if your business card stays visible to the person you handed it to, you could still miss out on valuable business. If you do not place contact information to all your social media sites on the card, you may be missing out on potential clients or customers. Corralling business cards into a medium that attracts business becomes more difficult each day.

What this book proposes to business owners are a number of ways to make a published book work for you while you are off gathering more leads. Opening doors is one of the great benefits to having a book. A book not only sets you up as an expert in your field, it also carries with it the capability of delivering value to your potential clients and customers.

While your competition hands out business cards, you can deliver 'take-home' information potential clients may use to better their lives. One of the catch-phrases you hear in marketing today is to give potential clients/customers something of value at no cost and you win their loyalty. For many businesses, a book becomes an excellent delivery method.

The ***Your Book as YOUR Business Card*** concept can be delivered to your audience in a number of formats, both digital and print. The following information could dramatically change the way you do business.

Marketing Tool

Information in ***Your Book as YOUR Business Card*** should include the full scope of your business, including every detail of your products and services. Keying on the high points and value you offer potential clients/customers should be one of the primary focuses of your book.

Include historical content, how you got to where you are today, and any graphics that might help convey positive energy toward what you do. To keep print costs to a minimum, use only graphics that look sharp in black and white. When you add color to the interior of print media like books and magazines, the costs can skyrocket.

Also include all social media contact information. Today, in the 21st century, business connections are surging through the use of social media, the three most popular being Facebook, Twitter, and LinkedIn. Adding your business to numerous social media marketing sites can fill an entire page, or even more.

Oversized Business Card

While business cards are still an important advertising tool, with ***Your Book as YOUR Business Card***, their purpose is more about being placed inside the book you hand your potential client. Business cards, by their minimal size, are limited in information they can display. Placed in a book like a bookmark, your business card has a much higher probability of being saved and used as a reference to a business opportunity.

Rich Content Business Cards Cannot Deliver

Most successful businesses fill a 'niche' need to a select customer base. Here is one of the most valuable tools ***Your Book as YOUR Business Card*** has to offer: Your opportunity to impart valuable information immediately in hand – and give your potential customer something of high value – free. That potential customer will be more inclined to call upon you and your business to answer questions.

For example, a Karate school may publish a small book offering free beginner technique information, with black and white pictures depicting the basic exercises necessary to the craft. Yoga schools, Personal Trainers, Dance schools, etc, are other examples of businesses that could use this marketing strategy.

Let's say you have a business that supplies home beer brewing equipment. Offer free recipes, techniques, and tips to help potential customers produce a quality product. When a potential customer sees the massive benefit given to them freely, goodwill is established, much more so than a simple business card and a forgotten face. That customer will be more inclined to visit your business for personal service.

Another example could be an accounting service that discusses valuable tax tips, accounting practices, and no nonsense tips on how to keep the ledgers in good shape. Many accounting service people give out tips and information along these lines daily. By placing valuable information in ***Your Book as YOUR Business Card***, you draw potential customers to you and away from the competition.

Book as a Prize

Everyone loves free, especially when *free* delivers unexpected value. Setting up contests and giveaways like charitable donations and silent auctions, you put your company and its products and/or services in the hands of potential clients. These giveaways not only put your information out for consumption, it also shows you care about the community enough to donate valuable material.

Income Stream/Marketing Tool

Many, if not most, businesses need to attend conferences, conventions, trade shows and leads groups. Other business related events stand out as prime opportunities to make connections with potential customers.

At these venues, the chance there will be competitors at the same event is high. This situation is ripe with opportunity for the entrepreneur who seizes the day. ***Your Book as YOUR Business Card*** succinctly compiles your business information as well as delivers quality content your prospective customers need or desire.

Giving strong, quality content is critical to making ***Your Book as YOUR Business Card*** a success. Be willing to give up some indispensable information that will help your clientele. Your follow up with quality content is heightened over simple business cards because you can ask the potential client if they had a chance to use the information on such-and-such page.

Specific conversations can connect you to memorable interactions solidifying a relationship. Relationship building is a cornerstone, not only to acquiring new business, but also to getting referrals and repeat business. Your book acts as a bridge forming relationships as well as connecting you and your customers.

Your Book as YOUR Business Card can also be an income stream. When you place high quality content in the book, you can then sell the book to recoup your advertising dollar. While the book is a great advertising expense write-off, selling the book may be an option to help defray those costs.

Speaking Engagements

One of the most significant aspects of ***Your Book as YOUR Business Card*** is the book opens doors to speaking engagements. When you speak in front of targeted potential clients, giving the book to potential customers as a take-away can be a huge benefit. People like to go home with material that offers them *meat*, something they can sink their teeth into and implement. When you deliver a book that accomplishes this, your chance for contact from that potential client escalates dramatically.

Books still open the door to speaking engagements, just as was true in years past. You may choose to incorporate the book as a sales item, but I would recommend it as a giveaway if you can afford to do it. If you are charging for your speaking services, simply incorporate the cost of the books you give out into the fee you charge to speak.

If someone else is coordinating the speaking engagement, offer them your book at cost and have them offer a **"Free Book With Paid Registration"** in your name. This helps them fill registration orders, gets you money to cover the cost of your book, and THEY can incorporate your "free" book in their pricing if need be.

You may want to do virtually the same thing with pre-registration situations, which today appears to be the way most events are organized. By coordinating with event promoters you can offer your book "free" with a pre-paid registration, then advertise something to the effect of "Books may be purchased for $x.xx on the day of the event." This allows you to cover the cost of the "free" books up front, and opens the possibility for book sales at the back of the room after you speak.

There are many ways books and speaking engagements go together. Gifting the event organizer and their people may be a way to negotiate the above scenarios. Remember, event planners are always looking for something they can *give* people to show up to an event. If you can help them out, you increase your positive *stock* with this event planner, which may get you referrals to other events as well.

Buy Product or Service – Get Book Free

"Buy Product or Service – Get Book Free" - while self explanatory, there may be interesting tweaks or add-ons you can incorporate. One such add-on would be a combination of products and book.

Let's say you manufacture spices for cooking. You put together a package deal with several of your special spices, a DVD of you cooking recipes using yours spices, and a cookbook with great recipes - detailing everything on the DVD as well as supporting your spices yet again. While this is not necessarily getting the book for "free," in a package deal like this, you could offer the cookbook as a free item if you buy the other two.

Coordinating your costs with what you charge in this situation, of course, is critical, but the perception of value in package deals like this is high. Tying your book to your product can be a huge benefit.

What about a service? Let's take a life coach or business coach. If you incorporate some of your coaching techniques in the book, tied directly to your coaching regimen, the book becomes very valuable. The book becomes a reincarnation of you when the client is *on their own*. Offering the book "free" to a client purchasing your services propels you to another level.

As s life or business coach, you could also set up a workbook as well, not to use as a business card, but to offer another level of service to your clients. This book would be something in which the client could journal, take notes and stay connected to the coaching process.

Buy the Book – Get a Discount

Similar to the "get a free book" above, depending on the prices of your product or service, you may want to give discounts to people who purchase the book online or at an event. This can be ENORMOUSLY effective as potential clients then feel like the book has added value beyond their purchase.

Let's say your book is so full of information that you want to charge $50 a copy. There are many industries where you have incredibly valuable information you do not wish to give away free. Once a client buys your book, if they go on to buy a product or service from you, let them know the $50 they spent on the book will go toward the purchase of the product or service.

Please remember the cost of printing your book will not be high. When you allow the client to credit $50 toward their purchase, your cost in the book is all you relinquish. In some instances, the print cost of your book may be only $2 to $5 per book – a small price to pay to get business on high-end products and services. Truly, a massively effective sales tool.

Writing Your Book

As mentioned numerous times, quality content is key to success with ***Your Book as YOUR Business Card***. The more information your client can use that you give away, the more likely they will be anxious to do business with you. This is equally true of products and services. I cannot stress enough the value of "giving something" to your prospective clients.

In this day of instant gratification as well as financial havoc, the entrepreneur/business owner, who steps forward and offers more value and personal service to prospective clients, will typically supersede businesses that offer less.

Before you begin, you must remember a very, very basic, important fact about writing – you must kick the critic to the curb. You do not write a *first draft* of your book worrying about grammar, punctuation, spelling or anything else. I'll get more into this a little later, just prepare yourself to write free of any internal judge.

Content is Key

Quality content. Quality Content. Quality Content. Have I stressed this critical aspect of the book enough? I hope so. Prospective clients want to go home with something they can use and incorporate into their business or lives. Too many times I have been teased by businesses offering great things only to get home and find I cannot use anything they gave me.

I am not proposing you give away the business, but you must have some aspect of your business with which you can help your potential clients. A common, everyday issue is one of the best "free" offerings you can make. The spice owner who cooks, mentioned earlier, can give away culinary tips all day long. That will not hurt his spice sales, nor the sales of his cookbook and DVD. In fact, this offers huge value to those who love to cook and prepare unique foods.

A karate school can offer basic beginner exercises, the history of their discipline and maybe even some basic moves with black and white photos or line art. While this does give away some of what the school most likely incorporates into their pricing already, there is no substitute for a live teacher. Giving away this information will not necessarily make the student a black belt, but it will endear the school to potential clients. In fact, the school could probably do a full, comprehensive book detailing the entire curriculum to black belt and still not lose any business.

Why? Because of expertise. If everyone could just read a book to become perfectly knowledgeable, or skilled, or adept at something, there would be no need for actual businesses focused on these things. The fully comprehensive book would then have huge value sales-wise as well as huge value to the student needing to practice or study. All the material would be right there in their grasp.

Presently, I am writing a book describing how to set up a publishing company and publish books. I am offering step-by-step guidance so that anyone can publish the book of their dreams. Why would I do this? Wouldn't I be potentially killing my business?

Absolutely not! Most people today do not have the time to take on something as complex as publishing, nor do they necessarily wish to take on the learning curves involved. So what is the value of this book then?

Many aspects of publishing happen piecemeal. Each *piece* has industry-wide associated costs. For example, there is editing, graphic design for book covers, interior art, and pagination and layout. Then follows distribution, royalties, trade discounts to retailers, returns and a myriad number of small items most folk would prefer not to have deal with.

While a business owner may be able to provide some of these aspects, perhaps in-house graphics designs, other aspects would be better served by outsourcing.

In the case of my book, I am giving away tons of valuable information. My book is priced accordingly. Some people will be able to read the book and incorporate all the complexities into a viable publishing company. Others will want some consultation, so I am offering paid webinars as well as one-on-one consulting.

All bases are covered. As a publisher, I am offering authors/writers various avenues to achieve that goal of getting their books out to the world in print or electronic form.

Painting your Business Portrait

Do not cut corners here. Your business had a beginning and people love to know how businesses started and progressed. People want to know about your challenges and the ways you overcame them. They are curious about your story. Customers want to know and feel that you can handle their needs. Connecting personally is the key.

Describe your business history from why the business started, how it grew and where it's at today. Keeping it chronological keeps the customer informed in a logical, easy to visualize manner.

Do not limit yourself to the history of your business. This section of your book is where you should shine. As you go through your history, incorporate any new products or services you added. Place these in appropriate areas of your history. You can place an appendix at the back of the book detailing your products and/or services in a cleaner, tidier format. People like to see how products and services came into being in a company.

In the history/products/services section, you also have opportunity to bring up specific struggles, challenges or hurdles you helped past and present clients overcome. People identify with struggles. When you present struggles you helped solve, potential clients are drawn to your ability to take care of your customers. That is what they are looking for: excellent customer service.

You should also incorporate a full range of contact information with reasons to choose one form over another. You may be on Facebook, LinkedIn, Twitter, StumbleUpon, Tumblr, and/or many other social media. Each form of contact delivers its own special brand of information.

You may encourage clients to get involved in forums you set up online or get into discussions on LinkedIn. You may run a blog and you may want to encourage clients to interact through taking polls or commenting on your blog. You may prefer to be contacted through the *message* aspect of Facebook. You may also prefer email and email direct marketing.

These days, using social media to your advantage can be a huge benefit. There are social media businesses out there that can help you set this up as well as maintain it for you if you like. I encourage you to look into social media as a means of marketing.

While certain businesses need to rely on telephone communication and a more personal direct connection, you can always direct your customers to seek more information on your social networking sites.

Writing the Innards

Many of us, myself included, hated outlines in school. My belief is this prejudice against the outline is totally unfounded and in fact, has hampered many of us for many years. When you get ready to write your content, please do yourself the biggest favor you could ever perform – draw up an outline of what you want in your book.

The writing will come much easier, you will remain more organized, and your end product will come out sensible and readable. I've been writing for thirty years, twenty of which I disdained the outline. Once I conceded the absolute value of an outline, my ability to produce a quality book skyrocketed.

Use the outline to your greatest advantage. Break your business down into outline topics and then use the outline to set up *chapters*. Chapters in a book this small do not have to be long. In fact, chapters of one or two pages create an easy reading environment for your customers.

Do not worry about page count or word count. In fact, don't worry about spelling, grammar or any of that *writing stuff*. Just write using your outline. You should target your book to run between 40 and 96 pages. Before those numbers intimidate you, let me demystify this for you a bit.

In a book, you will have what is called a "Title Page" which basically is the cover of your book in black and white. You don't have to write anything for that page. Look! You're already done with one page! Then there's the copyright page. If you are outsourcing this book rather than doing it yourself, the publisher will take care of this page for you. Two pages done!

Then there's the Table of Contents. This page cannot be completed until the book is written and you don't have to write anything new for this page. Depending on book length and number of chapters, you may have a couple pages in your TOC. You're up to four pages done and haven't written a word.

Then there's the author page or, I would suggest, Company Bio page. This page simply gives a quick overview of the company or the author. This is a simple page you can put together quickly because no one knows you or your business like yourself.

With a 50 page book, you are now left with 45 pages to write. Before this freaks you out, realize that each page of a 6 x 9 book will contain approximately 250 words. Forty five pages times two hundred fifty words is 11,250 words. Do you realize I write around two thousand words an hour and I am not particularly fast on a keyboard. At that rate, I could (and presently have with this book) complete a first draft of a book in around six hours.

"What?" you say, "Write a book in six hours?"

Ok, let me be realistic. You've spent time setting up your outline, thinking about all the stuff you want in your book and a few other things, I'm sure. Still, the actual writing does not take so long. Let's say you are very slow on a keyboard. Let's say I'm twice as fast.

It will take twelve hours of actual writing to get you to fifty pages. Literally, if you spent two hours a day writing, you could be done with the first draft in one week. Remember, this is your business you are writing about. No one knows it like you do. Maybe your biggest problem will actually be keeping the book under 96 pages. We all possess a lot of information that we do not realize we have. We take ourselves for granted far too much.

Before you think you are done, go back to the beginning of each chapter and write a paragraph telling the reader what you are about to tell them in the chapter. Then go to the end of the chapter and recap, basically telling the reader what you told them. Many of you may have heard the "tell them what you're going to say, then tell them, then tell them what you've said" method of getting information to stick with people. This is an effective way of helping your reader understand what you wrote as well as helping you get your page count up if you're coming in a bit short.

Remember I mentioned kicking the critic to the curb? Once you finish your first draft, find four to six people, preferably within your industry, who will volunteer to read through your book and mark any mistakes they find. Use these people for finding spelling and grammar errors, problems with how you may have worded something, and for feedback on how the book reads.

There is most likely more time spent in this *revision* process than the actual writing. I prefer *hard copies* where each person has a printed copy of the book and they mark their observations directly on the paper. This is, admittedly, an outdated way of doing things. In Microsoft Word there is a tool called "Track Changes" which allows people to go in and make changes to what you typed. A notation of the correction will be on the screen for you to accept or decline.

Just because a reader thinks something should be worded a particular way does not mean you have to go with their suggestion. The best rule of thumb with the revision and editing process is ***keep the best and throw away the rest***.

Once your *first readers* have returned their assessments of the book, make the changes you feel appropriate, then hire a professional editor. This will cost money. The industry standard for a decent editor is 1.5 cents per word. The great thing about a small book is, at 11,250 words you are only looking at an editing cost of around $170.

Yes, you can skip the editor, but I strongly recommend you spend the money. This book will be a reflection of you and your business. If you produce a book with a lot of typos and poor grammar, you and your business validation are questioned.

The great thing about the writing process is you do not have to be an expert in spelling or grammar. Your readers and editors will take care of that for you. One thing you must have is a thick skin. Whenever you write and someone comes behind you correcting things, you need to look at the input as making your book effective and legitimate, all the more powerful for potential customers - not that they are making negative personal statements about you.

One truth I hold onto during the revision process other than my book getting stronger, most of the people reading and editing your book have never written one themselves. Once you are done, you will have the sense of delightful accomplishment as well as a major tool to help your business grow.

I also recommend a dedication page that acknowledges all the people who helped you put the book together. This reflects well on you with potential clients that you give recognition to others, it helps you *repay* your readers for their *pro bono* work by getting their names in print, AND it adds another easy page to your book.

There are a number of great books out there on how to write a book from beginning to end. I like *Writing for Fun, Fame, and Fortune* by Rik Feeney. Mr. Feeney gives you a simple step by step guide on how to complete a book in basically thirty to forty days. For our purposes here, that time frame could easily be a couple weeks.

When you look for a professional editor, find someone with whom you feel comfortable. You will be communicating back and forth and you will need to foster a good working relationship. This especially comes into play when the editor recommends you change something you do not wish to change. You must be willing to listen to their expertise and willing to concede where appropriate.

By the same token, your editor will need to be amenable to your reluctance to accept all their suggested edits. This calls for a personality match where that environment can grow and produce good results.

Remember, it is the book that is the focus here, not the people. ***Your Book as Your Business Card*** - the primary objective is to increase and grow the business.

If you do not know how to find a good editor, find a small press publisher and ask who they use. Or go to a local writer's group and inquire as to who they know that edits books. Most writer's groups can steer you in the right direction.

I like the small publishing company the most, though. My company uses three editors and we refer work to these editors all the time. This is your easy button. I did have one author who found his editor online using Google. Instead of my recommendation of editors, he went with an editor in Arizona.

This author has now published two books and used the Arizona editor for both because they have a great working relationship. This is another aspect of this business that is wonderful. Your editor can be located just about anywhere because most editing is handled through online communication these days.

Book Layout

When setting up your book, layout determines what your finished product will look like. The fonts you use and the margins, graphics, and any visually aesthetic devices you may add all combine to give your book a *feel*. When you set the book up, you will determine the trim size of the book.

There are numerous book sizes in publishing today. For ***Your Book as YOUR Business Card***, a more compact size like 5"x8" may be preferable for most projects as it conjures the business card concept. Many paperback books these days run in the 6x9 trim size. By using the smaller size, you make transportation of your book simple, plus the book will stand out from the larger sized books.

Drawing attention to your products and services stands as the primary goal of ***Your Book as YOUR Business Card***. In this section of my book, I am going to give you some pointers on using Microsoft Word for laying out your book. Keep in mind, if you know how to use Adobe InDesign, this program allows a more professional layout experience.

Using Micorsoft Word can produce a quality book and as most people are more familiar with standard word processing programs, this is a valuable and reliable tool. I've produced over a dozen books using Word.

Getting Started

Once you've decided on the *trim size* of your book (5x8, 6x9, 8.5x11, etc), you may set Microsoft Word up for that print or trim size. You may want to wait until you've completed your manuscript in the 8.5x11 Word default size. Either way works. I'm going to switch from the 8.5x11 size I am currently using to write this book to 5x8 which will be the end product size. Word will reformat the text already written to fit the new size.

Go to the **Page Layout** tab. Click on the **Size** tab. Scroll to the bottom and click on **More Paper Sizes.** Manually type in 5" for the width and 8" for the height.

Click on the **Margin** tab. For this book I am changing the default margins from 1" all the way around (top, bottom, right, left) to .5". This will cut down on the unused space on the outer edges of the page. For a larger sized book, a one inch margin may work, but for one this size I feel the book 'layout' calls for smaller margins.

Before you move on, click on the **Gutter** size. For this book, I am going to set the gutter at .25". The gutter is the center of the book. If you do not set a gutter, your text may fall deep into the *gutter* formed when the book gets bound. This will make it difficult for readers to see the letters that fall into the gutter.

While you are in the Margin tab, keep the default **Portrait** orientation. The next item under orientation is **Pages**. You will note the words "multiple pages" with a drop-down menu beside it. Click on the drop-down and select **Mirror Margins**.

Now click on the **Layout** tab. I like to set my Headers/Footers as "different odd/even pages". This allows me to put the title of the book on say the odd numbered pages and my name as author on the even numbered pages. One thing I must watch here is I've set my margins at .5" and my Header/Footer default is .5". This will not allow any separation of my Headers from my text. I will set the Header/Footer size to .35".

Now I am ready to click "ok". Note in the bottom left corner there is a drop-down that is labeled "Apply to:" This drop-down defaults to **Whole Document** which is what I want. I want all the changes I've just set in Page Layout to apply to my entire document.

There are other things I can do to tweak the layout of the book. I like what is called *white space* when I read a book, especially one like this that delivers a lot of information. One way to create white space is to change the distance between the lines of text.

The default distance is 1.0 in Word. I am changing this book to 1.2. I prefer to make the change once I have my first draft complete. You may set this up in Word before you begin. The reason I wait is I like to get a visual when I make the change.

I press Ctrl-A to select my entire document. Then I right click and select **Paragraph**. I go down to the "Line Spacing" drop-down. I set the spacing at "single" and then next to that under the word "at:" I type 1.2. This spreads out the lines of text which makes the book easier to read.

One other tweak is the font size. I want this book to come in around 46 pages. Why 46? At this point in writing ***Your Book as YOUR Business Card***, I am at 28 pages. I should be able to wrap up the book in ten pages, leaving me blank pages for a title page, a copyright page, a table of contents and a dedication page along with an author page. The last page, as per my printer, must be blank.

I then have a couple pages to work with should I desire to add graphics. One reason someone may want to shoot for 50 pages stems from the fact that a book must be at least 50 pages to place it into the Library of

Congress. Note: A book does not have to be placed in the LOC to be published.

Other layout tips can be things like over-sizing the first letter of each chapter of your book. This takes a little manual tweaking, but the resulting view can give your book a subtle, more professional feel to the read.

Using different fonts to call attention to sub-heads or other text can spiff a book up a bit. For the purposes of **Your Book as YOUR Business Card**, content is the primary focus, so I'm not going to get too involved with *dolling* the book up.

Setting Color and Print Resolution

If you add graphics of any kind, the color settings **MUST** be set to CMYK (cyan, magenta, yellow, black). Most programs, like Word, default to RGB (red, green, blue). The big issue with RGB is there is no true black setting. Four-color printing also produces sharper images.

Another MUST setting is the print resolution. This setting must be 300dpi (300 dots per inch) to give a high-resolution reproduction of any pictures or graphics.

Even if all your images going into the book are in black and white, you still MUST set both of these to the proper print settings. CMYK and 300dpi. Remember, Word defaults to RGB even to print the color black.

Anything less than 300dpi will very likely give you a grainy look to the pictures or graphics.

By taking the time to set your book up and lay it out the way you want the book to look, you can save money. Graphics design people are very good at what they do, and they tend to charge accordingly.

Pagination

Pagination is closely related to layout. Pagination can be tedious work because it is detail oriented. Pagination is a much simpler process with programs like InDesign because Microsoft Word has a lot of issues with moving text around for unknown reasons. One of the most common instances is the first line on each page. The first line should ALWAYS start exactly in the same position on every page. Word will often shift a line down one line.

Readers may or may not notice, but their subconscious will notice. When the book is not perfectly uniform throughout, the reading experience can be diminished. Also, as you make edits and changes to text, this line-dropping can become more prevalent.

Chapter titles should ALL begin at the exact same spot on the page. If you choose one-third of the way down the page, you need to note the position and duplicate that exact spot on every chapter page.

Another pagination issue is *widows/orphans*. When you get to the bottom of a page, often a paragraph will end and the first line of the next paragraph will be the last line on the page. This is a *widow*. Tweaking your page to get that line on the next page makes your book look sharper.

Do not simply hit enter on your keyboard to achieve this. Hit Ctrl-Enter to give a page break. This will pay off when your book gets converted to PDF.

Pressing simply *Enter* gives you what is called a "hard return" which causes all kinds of formatting issues when attempting to get a book ready for print. Most instances of *hard returns* must be removed and corrected before a book is print-ready.

An *orphan* is when you turn a page and there is only a line or two of text. In the worst of cases, sometimes when you turn a page there is only one single word on the page due to it being the end of a chapter. Getting that word back on the previous page can take a little work, but can be done in Word. This is another reason InDesign is a better program with which to set up a book. InDesign is better equipped to handle these types of issues.

There are ways to tweak your text to rescue orphans. In Word, this can be a bit tricky. Please check out ClearView Press Inc's free white paper on **Pagination** for ideas.

Cover Design

Your book cover should reflect the content of your book without being overly busy. A straight-forward graphic presentation that tells potential readers at a glance what your book is about is invaluable to the book being purchased or read. I like constructive simplicity.

The colors of the cover of this book are tied to the colors in the website and marketing materials of. **ClearView Press Inc.** This is a form of *branding* that lets a customer know subconsciously that the book is a product of **CVP**. This also allows a customer to go to our marketing materials both online and in print and see a similarity of colors. This helps define or *brand* **CVP**.

On the cover of this book we see two hands exchanging a business card with the words "My Book" clearly visible on the card. The subtitle, *Your Book as YOUR Business Card*, is reinforced by the picture so there is no doubt about the content of this book. This is very important.

People do not like being tricked into reading something through false representation. If we placed a bikini-clad model on the cover, we might attract a certain element of the population to check the book out, but no one would purchase the book because the cover misrepresented what is inside.

Give your potential market the best opportunity to see what your book will give them. Potential clients also want to know "What's in it for me?" By delivering, with your title and cover graphics, a clear statement of what your book entails, you will better target your potential client/customer. Placing valuable information in your book, as stated earlier, is key to getting the most out of your ***Your Book as YOUR Business Card***.

Publishing Model

Here at **ClearView Press Inc.,** we offer our clients the publishing model for *Your Book as YOUR Business Card* with a 2000 copy print run. By printing 2000 copies, **CVP** is able to deliver a cost-effective price point to you the customer.

Large print runs offer an *'economies of scale'* aspect to the print costs. The more books you print in one print run, the lower the price per book. Two thousand copies afford an attractive price point to businesses. For less than $2.00 per book, you can deliver huge value to your customers, explain and layout your products/services, give a history of your company and deliver all the means by which your company wishes to be contacted.

Taken solely on this price point, **CVP's** package for *Your Book as YOUR Business Card* is competitive with local small printers. What the local small printer does not offer, though, is global distribution through online retailers around the world. Retailers like Barnes and Noble, Books A Million and Amazon. You may have a product or service that benefits people all over the country, hemisphere or world. Currently the Ingram Distribution System reaches the U.S, Canada, U.K,

European Union, Southeast Asia, and Australia. Brazil will soon be opening up as a retail market as well. All this is included with the ***Your Book as YOUR Business Card*** package.

CVP tracks sales through Ingram and pays royalties for any books sold throughout the world. Some businesses may not need global distribution, but U.S. only. U.S. distribution is obviously covered.

The main focus of ***Your Book as YOUR Business Card*** is to deliver a product to business owners that allows them to get a leg up on the competition. By delivering your business into potential client/customers' hands, you get a more powerful tool than a simple business card. You are delivering yourself and your company directly into the hands of those who need your product or service.

Re-orders

Another beneficial aspect of **CVP's** ***Your Book as YOUR Business Card*** package is a reduced price for re-orders. As long as no changes are made to your book, you can reorder another 2000 copies at a reduced price. Once a book is set up, it stays in the computer system. Re-orders are a simple phone call or email away.

Minor changes made to the book can be incorporated at nominal fees depending on their complexity which still allows for a price reduction on re-orders. If you have a price change on a couple products or services, most of these can be handled for a $75 fee. The business would still receive their price reduction for re-order.

One thing to remember on changes to a book, a revision must be sent by **CVP** to the printer. This can take up to a week to work its way through the printer's system. Once the printer updates their files with the changes, the book is then print-ready.

ClearView Press Inc. History

To give you the full history of **ClearView Press Inc**, I must go back to 1979. I was in college at West Virginia Institute of Technology in Montgomery, West Virginia. I was an accounting major.

I took Creative Writing as a sophomore. The professor, Pat Urbas, informed the class the first day that 75% of our grade would be a short story we would compose over the course of the semester. She also told us on the last day of class, she would read the best story aloud to the class.

After some internal groaning, I diligently worked on my story. The more I wrote, the more I found I enjoyed the whole writing experience. By the last day of class, I knew I had written a pretty good story.

Yes, she ended up reading my story aloud. I was mortified. Being a very shy person, I felt like everyone in the room was looking at me. It felt oddly thrilling and frightening to hear my story read to all these people.

After class, Ms. Urbas pulled me aside, despite my attempt to slip out quietly. She said something to me that I quote verbatim today. She said, "Mike, you should consider writing as a vocation."

I stood there, stunned. My only thought was, ***I'm an accounting major, not a writer***. Yet, from that moment on, I wrote. I wrote poetry, short stories and essays. For the next 20 years, I often said, "One day I will be a published author."

November 2, 1999. I nearly died on an operating table in Deland, Florida of peritonitis. The surgeon told me afterward that another 4 to 6 hours, I would have died.

It took me months to recover. During this recovery time, I realized that our "one days" never come. They do not 'just happen'. If you have a dream, you must pursue that dream to make it happen. With that commitment in my heart, I moved forward.

I dove into learning how you go about becoming a *published author*. During the twenty years I wrote in secret, I had managed a number of businesses in a number of industries. I had my B.S. Degree in Business Management. After a few years of studying the publishing industry, I learned the *traditional publishing* business model was beyond ridiculous.

The industry was weighted to the publishers – the writers got nothing. I could not abide by that. In 2007, I incorporated **ClearView Press Inc**. I decided I would be a *rage-against-the-machine* publisher. I would show writers how to put dollars into their pockets per book rather than the pitiful cents major publishers paid.

I published my first book in March 2008 titled *Fatherhood 101: Bonding Tips for Building Loving Relationships*. In 2009 came my second book, *Loves Lost and Found*. 2010 brought five new books (and authors). 2011 brought five more. In September 2011, I realized I could help entrepreneurs. I could hand them a win-win situation with ***Your Book as YOUR Business Card***.

Today, **ClearView Press Inc**. is dedicated to delivering win-win environments to authors, entrepreneurs and businesses. We prefer a personal touch with our publishing. We are the "Author Friendly" publisher because I believe there is a better business model than what is typically given by the large publishers.

At **ClearView Press Inc.**, we handle editing, layout, pagination, cover design along with the other publishing tasks like acquiring the copyright in the author's name, setting the book up in a global distribution system (Ingram), and handling sales/royalty tracking, etc.

Contact CVP

Michael Ray King has authored or co-authored six books as of this printing with a seventh book, *The Method Writers*, due out in April 2012. Mr. King writes poetry, short stories, novels, and non-fiction self-help books. ***Rock Your Business! Your Book as YOUR Business Card*** is the seventeenth book published by **CVP** .

ClearView Press Inc.
PO Box 353431
Palm Coast FL 32135

mrking@clearviewpressinc.com
Phone: 386-290-6908

Office located at:
405 N State Street
Unit #2
Bunnell FL 32110
Phone: 256-867-7468
Fax: 877-526-5210
cindyg@clearviewpressinc.com

Social Media:

CVP Website:	http://clearviewpressinc.com
Facebook:	https://www.facebook.com/ClearViewPress
Facebook:	https://www.facebook.com/pages/Loves-Lost-and-Found/241053629274692
Facebook:	https://www.facebook.com/MichaelRayKing
Other sites:	http://michaelrayking.com
	http://poetryinblackandwhite.com
	http://roguesgallerywriters.com
	http://themethodwriters.wordpress.com/
Linked-In:	www.linkedin.com Michael Ray King
Twitter:	https://twitter.com @ClearViewPress
Stumbleupon:	http://www.stumbleupon.com/stumbler/MichaelRayKing
Hub Pages:	http://michaelrayking.hubpages.com

Books Published by ClearView Press Inc.

Motherhood is Easy	by Rebekah Hunter Scott
Saint Augustine Carriage Tour	by Phil King
Terrorcruise	by Charles Brass
Earth Cell The Ux-Blood Trilogy Part 1	by Charles Brass
Freeing Unconditional Love	by Susan Marion
Bearding the Lion That Roared: The Levinson Cornerstones in Organizational Consulting Psychology	by Dr. A. M. O'Roark
Reflections and Watercolors	by Dr. A. M. O'Roark
The Accidental Diet From Fugly to Fox	by Alicia Hunter

*Books by **Rogues Gallery Writers:***

Writing is Easy
More Writing is Easy
The Method Writers (pending)

*Books by **Michael Ray King:***

Fatherhood 101: Bonding Tips for Building Loving Relationships
Loves Lost and Found
Poetry in Black and White
Rock Your Business!
Your Book as YOUR Business Card

From **Out of Your Mind Publishing LLC** (CVP Imprint)

Which Really Came First? Creation or Evolution	William B. C. Parnell
Life is Good! A Personal Journey (pending)	Richard C. Hébert